W9-BYK-308

The
Bitch
at
Work

ELIZABETH HILTS

SOURCEBOOKS HYSTERIA™
AN IMPRINT OF SOURCEBOOKS, INC.®
NAPERVILLE, ILLINOIS

Copyright © 2007 by Elizabeth Hilts
Cover and internal design © 2007 by Sourcebooks, Inc.
Cover illustration © Stephanie Piro
Internal illustration © Stephanie Piro
Sourcebooks and the colophon are registered trademarks of
Sourcebooks, Inc.

All rights reserved. No part of this book may be reproduced in any
form or by any electronic or mechanical means including information
storage and retrieval systems—except in the case of brief quotations
embodied in critical articles or reviews—without permission in writing
from its publisher, Sourcebooks, Inc.

Published by Sourcebook Hysteria, an imprint of Sourcebooks, Inc.
P.O. Box 4410, Naperville, Illinois 60567–4410
(630) 961–3900
Fax: (630) 961–2168
www.sourcebooks.com
ISBN-13: 978-1-4022-0971-0
ISBN-10: 1-4022-0971-1

Library of Congress Cataloging-in-Publication Data

Hilts, Elizabeth.
  The Bitch at Work / Elizabeth Hilts.
    p. cm.
  ISBN-13: 978-1-4022-0971-0 (trade pbk.)
1. Women in the professions—Attitudes. 2. Assertiveness in women.
3. Women—Life skills guides. I. Title.

HD6054.H54 2007
650.1082—dc22
                                    2007015960

Printed and bound in the United States of America
VP 10 9 8 7 6 5 4 3 2

Dedication

This book is for all the women who know that success is not a one-size-fits-all proposition. And for my precious girls, Shannon Hector and Cassidy Elizabeth Singleton, who inspire me to try to do my best work every day.

Taking Care of Business, Inner Bitch Style:

If it's true that you start being called a bitch only when you're successful, then maybe the best place to tap into the power of your Inner Bitch is at work. Or at home. Or wherever it is you most want to succeed.

Introduction

*C*ongratulations! You've taken the first step in tapping into the power of your Inner Bitch. Yes, just by picking up this book, you're on the way to creating success for yourself.

What does the Inner Bitch have to do with success? Well, everything. Let me explain.

In my first book, *Getting in Touch with Your Inner Bitch,* I exposed Toxic Niceness—the mysterious malady that drives us to self-defeating behavior, the only cure for which is getting in touch with your Inner Bitch. Toxic Niceness goes by a couple of aliases: "the disease to please," co-dependency, nurturing (which is fine in moderation, but which can be Toxic Niceness in sheep's clothing). No matter what you call it, when we suffer from Toxic Niceness everyone else in our lives gets more out of our efforts than we do. Toxic Niceness makes us say "yes" when we want to say "no." We eat a piece of cake (or even a whole cake) instead of giving someone a well-deserved piece of our minds. We apologize for things that are not our fault. Being in touch with our Inner Bitch, on the other hand, means calling it as we see it and never being afraid to speak our minds. The Inner Bitch is that part of ourselves that is smart, confident, and dignified. She knows what she wants, and she isn't willing to settle for less—which has *everything* to do with success.

Naturally, Toxic Niceness is lethal to relationships, a discovery that led to my second book, *The Bitch in the Bedroom*.

So this book was inevitable. After all, what else are you going to do with all that energy that you used to devote to taking care of everyone else? You might as well put it to work in the workplace, tapping into the power of the Inner Bitch to become as successful as possible. And your Inner Bitch wants you to dream big when it comes to this (and every) part of your life.

The trick is figuring out exactly what success means to you. Because let's face it, "one-size-fits-all" doesn't work with success any more than it does with clothes.

The Good News

Your Inner Bitch will help you find the way to move beyond the stumbling blocks that stand in the way of success—however you define it.

How do I know this? I know this because everything I have today I owe to getting in touch with my Inner Bitch. Besides the obvious, being in touch helped me get honest with myself about the road mines that impeded my path to success—stumbling blocks that, in some cases, I planted myself. For example:

❋ I had a hard time admitting that I'm ambitious—this was, of course, part and parcel of the way Toxic Niceness operated in my life.

❋ I was involved with people who didn't support my efforts—in my case, this group included my then husband, coworkers, bosses, and friends, some of whom actively discouraged me from pursuing success.

❋ For a long time, I was in the wrong career, which for me was a choice powerfully influenced by Toxic Niceness. Because I was so invested in making sure that everyone around me was taken care of, it took me a long time to realize that going to work every day was just misery, and not just because I had to wear pantyhose every day.

When I finally started to get in touch with my Inner Bitch, those road mines began to disappear. It wasn't magic; it took a lot of hard work.

But my point is this: I'm speaking to you from the trenches here. I don't have an MBA; I haven't climbed any corporate ladders; the only thing I'm an expert in is the Inner Bitch—and I promise you that being in touch with your Inner Bitch will help you find the success you really want.

How? Why, with a handy catchphrase, of course. *Getting in Touch with Your Inner Bitch* employed the phrase "I don't think so" (really, such an all-purpose phrase); *The Bitch in the Bedroom* used "What am I thinking?" (which beats "what was I thinking?" any day of the week). In keeping with the Inner Bitch tradition, to help you on your way, the handy catchphrase for the *The Bitch at Work* is "I'll think about that."

"I'll think about that" can work for us in a number of ways:

- It's a great alternative to saying "yes" to every request that comes your way.

✣ It gives you some breathing space before you formulate a definitive response.

✣ It makes you look like you've got your eye on the "big picture."

✣ It's simple to use.

Let's explore, shall we?

Success will not attack you.
You must attack success.

Chapter One
The Question of Success

*H*ow does the Inner Bitch define success? Let us count the ways!

According to the dictionary (*Webster's Third New International*, in this case), the definitions of success include:

1. The degree or measure of attaining a desired end
2. A kind of fortune
3. Succeeding fully or in accordance with one's desires
4. The attainment of wealth, position, esteem, favor, or eminence

That all sounds good, doesn't it? The only problem is that none of it is particularly helpful for this one, simple reason: defining success is a one-off, it's singular, and it's a custom job. Each one of us must define it for ourselves and—here's the kicker!—that definition is bound to change as we evolve. Even if we carve a definition of success in stone, the passage of time and the accumulation of experience are going to wear away the letters and leave us with a blank slate.

Isn't that just great?

"I don't think so," I hear you thinking. But stay with me here, I'll show you what I mean.

"*Before you can score you must first have a goal.*"

—Proverb

At one point in my life, I defined success as being able to pay my rent and still have money left over for groceries, gas, and a couple of pairs of pantyhose (which, believe it or not, were part of the dress code for women at that job) every month (the utilities got paid every other month), and I learned how to make those delicate pantyhose last through countless wears and the oh-so-inevitable runs.* A little later, the definition morphed slightly: success meant getting a job that didn't require the pantyhose. Fast forward a few years, and my definition of success had expanded to include an office with a door, direct reports (and a couple of indirect reports, as well), enough money to pay the mortgage, the car loan, and the cleaning service; buy groceries, gas, a new outfit just because I wanted one,

---

* Find two pairs of pantyhose, each with a run in one leg. Cut off the legs with runs and double up the pantyhose. Not comfortable, but effective in a pinch.

rounds of drinks, and a bunch more stuff; plus money to spring for a vacation, dinners out, theater tickets, and similar expenses.

Now my definition of success is a little bit more pared down: I can pay the mortgage and the cleaning service, and no one reports to me except the cat (and she, apparently, hasn't gotten that memo). I wear pantyhose only when absolutely necessary. Plus, I have the time to write books and enjoy my husband, my family, and my friends.

Which one is the right definition? All of them. As my life has changed, so has the meaning of success. And, if you think about it, so has yours.

Success—A Moving Target

Chances are you don't want the same thing now that you wanted five years ago. Perhaps that's because you've successfully attained the goal you set for yourself back then. Or maybe in the course of pursuing that goal, you learned about some new thing and shifted your focus a bit. It's even possible that you realized that you didn't even *want* that job, degree, or lifestyle you were putting so much energy into pursuing. Whatever the reason, what you want now is different.

Changing your goal doesn't mean that the goal you wanted so much wasn't worth working toward. It simply means that your dreams have changed, probably because you've reinvented yourself in the process of pursuing your goal. Even if the goal hasn't changed, you have.

"All mortals tend to turn into the things they are pretending to be."

—C.S. Lewis.

The truly important thing about defining success is that it helps us to dream big (and your Inner Bitch wants you to dream big). If we don't know what success looks like, is it possible to attain it? I don't think so.

There are, however, some obstacles we may encounter along the way.

Was That a Pothole?

Some of the road mines on the path to success are circumstantial, some are deeply rooted in "tradition," and still others are creations of our own making. Let's take a look, shall we?

Toxic Success

What could be toxic about success? Well, to begin with:

- Success by other people's definition is Toxic Success.

- Success that's limited to only one area of our lives, leaving the rest of it in a shambles, is Toxic Success.
- Success that looks wonderful from the outside but leaves you miserable is Toxic Success.

Need we go on? Toxic Success is as debilitating as Toxic Niceness ever could be. Your Inner Bitch wants you to make sure the success you choose is the success you really want, that the goal you pursue is the one you desire—not what your mom wants for you, or the one your boss has set as the basis for your next bonus or promotion.

Unequal Pay (Still)

Women and men still aren't being paid equal pay for equal work. "Oh, that can't be right," you may say. But it's true, and here are the statistics: In 1963, when the Equal Pay Act was passed, women who worked full-time were paid 59 cents on average to the dollar received by men. In 2004—41 years later!—women working full-time got 76 cents for every dollar paid to men. (Do the math: the wage gap narrowed by less than half a penny per year.) The gap is even worse for women of color: African American women received only 69 cents, Latinas just 58 cents.

According to NOW (the National Organization for Women), "If women were paid as much as men who work the same number of hours, have the same education and union status, are the same age, and live in the same region of the country, then women's annual income would rise by $4,000 per person, and poverty rates would be cut in half. Working families would gain an astounding $200 billion in family income annually."*

Outraged yet?

* National Organization for Women website. April 25, 2006.

The Glass Ceiling

They named it, but we don't have to claim it.

The truth is, however, that pretending the glass ceiling doesn't exist is silly. It's there, and so we have to deal with it. Oh, sure, there are women who have broken through and made it to the top—Carly Fiorina, Meg Whitman (CEO of eBay), Mickey Siebert (the first woman to purchase a seat on the NYSE), and maybe a few others come to mind; but 90 of the Fortune 500 companies don't even have women officers.

Another major stumbling block in the way of our success, however, is the thing we won't say out loud.

The Things We Won't Say Out Loud

There's an old saying that "we're only as sick as our secrets."

The reasons we don't say these things out loud are myriad, ranging from embarrassment to peer pressure to social imprinting (which is a fancy name for the things we learned growing up.)

What are these things of which we must not speak? Here are some of the prime examples:

"I'm ambitious."

What is it about this statement that makes us break out in a cold sweat? Actually saying those words out loud seems, well, unwomanly somehow. Even the women who have risen to the top of their fields downplay the role ambition has played in their success. "Oh, sure, I've won two Oscars and countless other awards, but this is just my day job. I'd really rather just be at home with my kids, mucking around in the garden, and baking cookies every day." Right. That's why I cheered when I saw this exchange between Felicity Huffman and Lesley Stahl on *60 Minutes* (January 15, 2006).

Lesley Stahl asks Huffman whether mother-hood is the best experience in her life. The reply is deemed "surprising." Here's what she said:

"No, no; and I resent that question," Huffman says. "Because I think it puts women in an untenable position because, unless I say to you, 'Oh, Lesley, it's the best thing I've ever done with my whole life,' I'm considered a bad mother. And just when I said 'no,' you went back."

How great is that? The bottom line is that Felicity Huffman is actually voicing an idea that a lot of us shy away from admitting even exists—that even if we value being mothers, our work can matter just as much (or maybe—gasp!—even more). Which leads us to this: *"My career success is at least as important as my personal success, and maybe more so."*

And this: *"I'm afraid that if I don't put my family first, people will think there's something wrong with me."*

On the surface these two statements might seem contradictory. Look a little deeper, however, and you'll see that they aren't really—and not just because they are things we don't say out loud.

"I've had to choose between my career and relationship/marriage/kids."

The truth is that success requires some sacrifices. After all, there are only so many hours in a day. If you're a single woman working full-time and going to school, there's probably not a lot of time for dating and hanging out with your friends. If you're a married mom who works full-time, things like "girls' night out" are probably rare events. No matter what your situation is, your pursuit of success (whatever that means to you) is going to cut in to some other areas of your life.

For instance, consider this quote from Becca Swanson—the Strongest Woman Alive (she can lift more than 2,050 pounds!) in *Pink* magazine: "Success Secret. Sacrifice. I had to forgo children. I would like to be married, and after ten years it's ridiculous that we're (she and business partner/ fiancé Rick Hussey) not, but all our finances go into the gym and all our time into lifting."* This is a woman who bought a gym while she was still in college and who puts in fourteen hours a day.

"I'm embarrassed by my desire for success and everything that means."

There seems to be some lingering belief that there's something wrong with a woman who is ambitious, who puts her career first, who wants—and works hard for—all the obvious trappings of success. If that weren't true, why would sitcoms (some of which are written by and star women) still get so much mileage out of making fun of ambitious women? Not to mention all the TV dramas, books, and movies that portray such women as cold-hearted bitches who lead lives that are ultimately meaningless, just waiting for someone to come along and save them from themselves.

* "Move over, Arnold." *Pink* magazine, Nov. 2006, 28

"Part of the reason I haven't put my career first is that my partner isn't as supportive as I need him to be."

Hmm. Perhaps this is a good time to revisit a pertinent idea first set forth in *The Bitch in the Bedroom*. To wit, a man who will not help you get to the top certainly isn't going to help keep you there. (This is not simply shameless self-promotion; it's leveraging existing assets, honey.) While one part of your Inner Bitch says, "Kick him to the curb," several other parts understand that this may not be the most reasonable solution. Your Inner Bitch also knows that if your partner isn't as supportive as you need him to be, the first thing to do is do a quick Toxic Niceness check. Are you asking for what you need, or have you fallen into the trap of thinking that your partner is a mind reader? Another question to ask yourself is this: what does *support* mean? Speaking from personal experience, I'll admit that for a long time I expected my husband (a.k.a. The Total Package) to support me by doing half the housework because I find that kind of thing drains my energy. And I was furious when I realized that he just wasn't going to. "Listen, I have deadlines to meet and meetings to prepare for and yadda, yadda, yadda. The least you could do is clean the bathroom and vacuum every other week!" I hollered at him. He pointed out, reasonably enough, that he also had a full plate to deal with.

As I continued to rant and rave about how overworked I was, the pressure I was feeling, and the unfairness of it all, he stopped me short with this simple statement: "I'm not trying to undermine you; I simply don't have the time."

That's when I hired a cleaning service. Because I realized that the important thing was freeing up my time, not making him do half the housework. Oh, and making sure the bathroom got cleaned.

My point is, "support" takes a lot of guises, and it can be found in a number of different places. Your Inner Bitch wants you to make sure you aren't cheating yourself of the support you need by insisting that it come from only one source.

"Career? I don't want a stinkin' career; I just need a job so I can keep body and soul together."

Not much to quibble with on this one. And most of us who feel this way are pretty willing to actually say so out loud. Your Inner Bitch says "Bravo." She also knows that if you're going to have to go to work, you might as well get the most you can out of the experience. So keep on reading.

Your Inner Bitch would like to remind you that not every question requires an immediate answer.

Chapter Two
"I'll Think about That"

So, how will "I'll think about that" help us get past the stumbling blocks on the way to success?

Let's Think about That

Your Inner Bitch wants you to reap all the benefits of your hard work—and let's be clear about this one thing: part of the reason they call it "work" is because it's hard, at least part of the time. Even jobs we love can try our patience, put us through the wringer, and drive us to distraction. Sound familiar? Sure it does; it's sort of like our relationships.

As in relationships, part of being in touch with your Inner Bitch in the workplace means knowing what you want, knowing what you're willing to do to get what you want, and acting accordingly. This is where "I'll think about that" really comes in handy.

Let's give it a shot, shall we? You'll want to begin using "I'll think about that" in small increments. For example:

✻ You're in the fourth strategy meeting this week and it's only Wednesday. At the first three, you've volunteered to research how five different things can be accomplished *and* offered to bring in donuts every day. The executive vice president (EVP) of Big Ideas wonders aloud if it would be possible to turn back time and get some more of the chocolate-covered crullers. Everyone in the room looks at you. "I'll think about that," you say, as you finish off the last cruller and lick the smudges of ganache off your fingers.

Okay, I know that's ridiculous. You don't eat crullers! But the point is that, if you're the one everyone looks at every time the EVP has one of those Big Ideas, then it's time for you to start applying "I'll think about that" at least three times a meeting. Because, darling, you've been bringing your Toxic Niceness to work with you, and the number of things you're researching proves that everyone else is getting more out of your efforts than you are. Let's not even talk about why you'd volunteer to bring donuts to work when you don't even eat them.

Of course, there will be times when you're asked to do something that really is necessary, but you need to buy yourself a little time. "I'll think about that" will definitely work in this situation.

✳ "Say, Clarice, how about you go talk to that Hannibal Lechter guy and find out if he can shed any light on this situation."

"I'll think about that, but first I've got to do some research on that other project I'm working on."

✳ Your boss drops by your cubicle to ask you if you can assist your coworker, Barry, with something because "the poor guy is overwhelmed."

You know that Barry is overwhelmed at having to choose what to have for lunch everyday. You also know from experience that assisting him means you do all the work and he gets all the credit. Besides, you already have enough work on your desk to keep you busy until, oh, two months from now—all of which needs to be done by Monday.

You can either go postal or try this approach. "I'll think about how I can get that done, but let me ask you this: is there anything I'm already working on that can wait until after this project is finished?" The beauty of putting the decision on the boss is that not only are you not refusing to help, you're asking for her help in prioritizing the department's workflow.

✳ While at lunch with a client, she hands you the prospectus for her son's latest business venture. "It's a great idea, and he's looking for investors. I'm putting in $10,000; you should, too!"

Your response: "I'll think about that." Once again, not really an answer, although your Inner Bitch wants you to carefully read the prospectus and consult with your financial advisor before making an investment. The added benefit of talking to your financial advisor is that, if you decide not to invest in your client's son's venture, you can blame the choice on an expert.

✳ One day you get a call from a recruiter who's trying to fill a position that just happens to be your dream job. "Know anyone who would be a good candidate?" she asks. "I'll think about that and get back to you tomorrow," you say.

Why wouldn't you just say, "Sure! Me! I'd be a

great candidate!" I'm glad you asked. The truth is she already knows you're perfect for the job, or she wouldn't have called you. And your Inner Bitch doesn't ever want you to jump first, think second. Besides, this gives you a chance to get all your little ducks into their little rows. Before you call her back, you'll have gotten your resume updated, have a list of all the reasons you'd be good for the job ready and (most important) you'll be making the call on your terms, not hers. (By the way, if you work in a cubicle, this will also give you an opportunity to make the return call from a more private location. If you have an office, you can shut the door.)

"I'll think about that" works. Odds are that if you give yourself a few minutes to think about the possible applications of it in your own life, you'll have a pretty long list.

Expanding the Scope

Of course, even the handiest catchphrase only goes so far, and once you've started calling on your Inner Bitch you'll clear the decks of those toxic time and energy drains. At that point you can begin to leverage the power of your Inner Bitch to start building the foundations of success your way by focusing on:

* Planning your work—This goes beyond just figuring out a schedule for accomplishing tasks. When you're in touch with your Inner Bitch, you'll be able to decide what it is you really want to do to keep body and soul together. Your Inner Bitch will broaden your career possibilities: whether you want to build your own business, change careers completely, or simply keep the job you have now.

* Building your team—Whether you're a manager or not, your Inner Bitch knows you need a team in order to succeed. And that

team has to include people you work with every day as well as people "on the outside."

✳ Handling mistakes—Your Inner Bitch knows that we learn more from our missteps than we do from success.

✳ Dealing with conflict—Really, who is more qualified for this particular task than your Inner Bitch?

✳ The Big Picture (a.k.a. Work-Life Balance)— Your Inner Bitch knows that all work and no play makes life one-dimensional, never mind making that guy Jack a dull boy. Are you willing to settle for a one-dimensional life? I don't think so.

✳ Being the boss—As I always say, when you're the boss, you're the bitch (the important part of that statement is that you are the boss) and success by any definition hinges on how you manage everything that entails: the power, the prestige, and the responsibility. Your Inner Bitch wants you to embrace the whole enchilada.

✽ Building the future you want—Ultimately, the point of being in touch with your Inner Bitch is having the life you really want, professionally and personally.

The point is, applying a good swift "I'll think about that" will clear the decks and make success, however you define it, much easier to attain.

Your Inner Bitch wants you to make sure that your career ladder is leaning against the right wall.

Chapter Three
Plan Your Work, Work Your Plan

*C*onsidering that we spend the majority of our day at work, in an ideal world we would enjoy what we're doing during those long hours. Your Inner Bitch knows that you don't live in an ideal world. She also knows that this simple fact doesn't mean you should settle for a job that doesn't satisfy you at least a little bit.

Dream a Big Dream

When she was a young girl, about ten, my friend Peggy decided that she wanted to be an astronaut—

primarily because in those days there were no female astronauts, so everyone told her she couldn't be one. Peggy did a little research and found out that most astronauts were good at things like science and math, plus they tended to know how to fly; so she spent a lot of time studying anything that had to do with the cosmos and doing complex algebra "for fun."

The good news is that all of Peggy's hard work paid off. Because of her deep knowledge and amazing grades in science and math, she got a full scholarship to a major university. And when her parents realized that she was really serious about trying to achieve her dream, they gave her flying lessons for every birthday and Christmas starting when she was sixteen.

What's it like to be an astronaut? You'll have to ask someone other than Peggy. During her sophomore year, she got a job working on an organic farm and realized that this was her real passion.

She switched her major to environmental studies, and now she has her own farm where she grows all kinds of healthy stuff. Recently she decided to learn how to make cheese. "It's ironic, I suppose," she says. "I thought I was headed for outer space, and here I am firmly planted on the Earth. But at least I'm using all that science!"

Does this make Peggy less than successful? I don't think so. She is, after all, doing what she loves—a good thing, considering how many hours she works—she lives in a beautiful place; and she still gets to fly every once in a while.

Of course, not everyone is as lucky as Peggy. For one thing, few of us figure out what we're really passionate about at such a young age. The simple truth is that many of us end up in jobs and professions almost by accident: We need to make a living, someone offers us a job, and we take that job. Sometimes we like the job, sometimes we don't—but what's a girl to do?

Well, your Inner Bitch wants you to think about that, and consider your options.

Consider Your Options

For example, when I realized (after seven years, by the way) that being a legal secretary wasn't exactly the career of my dreams, I bolted. Yep, I just left a perfectly good job that paid well and had benefits to become (drum roll, please!) *a writer.* My decision worked out okay ultimately, but if I'd been a little more in touch with my Inner Bitch, I might have done things differently, like Joan did.

Fresh out of high school, Joan got a job as a receptionist at a fairly large local company, which suited her just fine because she hated school and didn't even want to think about going to college. Eventually Joan ended up as the assistant to the president of the company, which, again, suited her just fine because she was making good money, she liked the guy, and the work was actually pretty easy most of the time. Joan answered the phone, scheduled appointments, ordered lunch, made some travel arrangements. In fact, Joan was kind of bored. "Some days I'd bring in a book, or I'd spend half my time on the phone with another executive assistant who was going through a rough time personally," she admits. Of course, Joan has always been the person her friends turn to for advice because she's very in touch with her Inner Bitch, and she's famous for telling it straight.

It was during one of those phone calls that Joan had an epiphany. "She said that I was giving her better advice than her therapist, and this light bulb went on," Joan told me. "I loved helping people sort out their problems, and I was, apparently, good at it. Eventually the president was going to retire, and what if I didn't like the next one? Would I even have a job in that situation? I figured it was time to explore my options, so after I hung up I called the local university and asked them to send me a catalog."

Joan perused the catalog, realized that the university offered a degree program designed for older students, and the very next day called the human resources department about the company's tuition reimbursement policy. "They paid 100 percent, but only if you got an A," she explained. Joan signed up for classes that very day and spent the next five years getting her degree. She did most of her studying at work and she graduated summa cum laude with a 4.0 average. Then she got into a post-graduate program for a master's in social work, which she also completed while employed. One year into that, the president of the company told her he'd be retiring the next year. Joan left the same day he did, to start her own practice as a therapist.

"Okay, fine," you say. "All these women love their jobs; every other woman knows what she really wants to do. Me, I just need to keep my job so I can continue to live my lavish lifestyle. But that doesn't mean I like it. So what am I supposed to do?"

Good question. Your Inner Bitch knows that we don't all end up in our dream jobs, and she also knows that some of us just don't want to put that much energy into our careers because we'd rather expend our efforts in different parts of our lives. But she does want you to be as content as possible, so she would like you to consider what works for your life.

What Works for Your Life?

My friend Dawn spent most of her adult life working at jobs that, for lack of a better term, "presented" themselves to her. She worked in retail, sold ad space for a newspaper, went back to retail, then she moved to California and somehow ended up being a freelance makeup artist working on TV shows, photo shoots, and the like. Being a makeup artist was a dream job for Dawn, and she loved it, but her personal life was . . . well, less than satisfying, so she moved back East and got a job as a recruiter. This job, in her words, "paid the bills" while she focused on building the life she really wanted, which included getting married and having a baby.

Imagine her surprise when, shortly after returning from maternity leave, Dawn realized that working full-time at a job that leaches out of the standard nine-to-five workday was no longer a good match for her. In a classic "good news, bad news" scenario, her boss also realized that fact and let her go—the good news being that Dawn no longer had to juggle the demands of work and a new baby, the bad news being (obviously) that she was unemployed.

However, being a resourceful woman, Dawn found a new job working as a teacher's assistant at a local elementary school. "It's not great money, but it has benefits," she told me. "Most important, it works for me and my family. After all, I waited until I was forty to have a child, and I want to spend as much time as possible being with her."

Your Inner Bitch knows that putting work in its proper perspective is vital—part of dreaming big, after all, is making sure that your whole life is as close to ideal as you can make it. So there's nothing wrong with having a job that enables you to focus on other areas of your life. In fact, that might just be ideal for you. The point of success, after all, is that each one of us has to define it for ourselves.

Your Inner Bitch knows that your ability to get things done at work depends to a large degree on other people, so it pays to get along with those other people. Does that require Toxic Niceness? I don't think so. But remember that a little give and take goes a long way.

Chapter Four
Your Team, Your Work

Give and Take

As someone once wrote, "Power is built on teamwork—think of the Sistine Chapel. Teams are built of individuals. The stronger the individuals, the stronger the team." Your Inner Bitch wants you to build yourself a strong team. Without a team you can't succeed, and she knows that your ability to get things done at work depends to a large degree on other people.

"*Teamwork divides the task and multiplies the success.*"

—That wise woman, Anonymous

Your Inner Bitch wants you to make sure that your team isn't made up just of people who are actually in your department, because in most workplaces we don't just work with people in our departments. In fact, we need to have good strong relationships with people throughout the organization. That way when we need to get something done, we can turn to our team members to help make it happen.

Who should be on your team? Glad you asked.

Team Members

"Go-To Gal"

We've all seen it happen: You're in a meeting, and someone relatively high on the office food chain says something like, "So, what if we tried something like this?" The "this" could be anything from ordering lunch to launching a new product; it doesn't really matter because "this" is an idea that comes from higher up. Silence descends as everyone stares studiously at their notepad or suddenly has to retrieve their hastily dropped pen from the floor. Everyone, that is, except than the "Go-To Gal."

You know her. She's the one who always volunteers to do the thankless busywork jobs, the one whose desk has neat piles of the paperwork and files that she needs as background for all that busywork, the one who acts as a kind of office mom. She's also the one who can't figure out why she hasn't been promoted in four years. "I give and give and give, do everything everyone asks me to do, why aren't they recognizing my contribution?"

You know the answer. She's too valuable in the position she has. If she were promoted, she wouldn't have the time to get all that busywork done!

The Go-To Gal, much like Nature, abhors a vacuum. While everyone else is carefully avoiding making eye contact with the other people in the room, she is waving her hand. "I can do that!" she says, eagerly. The higher-up nods, everyone else starts breathing again, and the Go-To Gal adds yet another task to her long, long list.

If you are the Go-To Gal, your Inner Bitch wants you to take a deep breath before volunteering.

If you are not the Go-To Gal, make sure she's permanently on your "Invite to Meeting" list (although you may want to consider giving her a copy of this book, because as Louisa May Alcott once said, "'Help one another' is part of the religion of sisterhood." And clearly, this sister needs some help).

The Juggler

That woman typing madly while holding the phone to her ear using some kind of weird yoga? She's a Juggler.

The one who is able to pull just the right

document out of her files while she's answering someone else's question? Yep, another Juggler.

How about that coworker who can juggle four projects with overlapping deadlines, hits every due date, takes Pilates during her lunch break so her workout doesn't interfere with her family life—and is always cool, calm, and collected? She just might be a Master Juggler. (She also may be taking some kind of mood-altering drugs, but, hey! if that's what works for her. . . .)

At first glance, Jugglers might be those women we love to hate and hate to love. The simple truth, however, is that every strong team needs one.

The Multi-Asker
No, not Multi-Tasker. As the name implies, the Multi-Asker does nothing without doing thorough research. Assign her a task and watch the questions fly! "Do you want that in an Excel spreadsheet? Didn't I do something just like this just last

month? Can't we use the existing data? What about making other people do parts of this and I'll just pull the information together at the end?"

"Let me think about that," you reply. Ten seconds later you hear yourself saying something like, "How about you just do it because it's your job?"

Of course, once in a while the Multi-Asker actually comes up with a good question, and while they may drive us a little nuts with all their questions, they may just be providing a valuable service. For instance, I once worked with a Multi-Asker—I'll call her Mary—who used the technique very effectively. During meetings the vice president of our group would often mention in passing that we'd been assigned yet another project.

"So who's going to come up with the schedule for that?" Mary would ask.

"Um, well, I guess the project manager?" the VP would say.

"And should we pull some people off the other ten projects we're already working on?" Mary would press on. "Or do you think we can just slip this into our existing workload?"

"I think I'll let the project manager take care of deciding that."

"Shall I call the project manager in to discuss how we're going to manage this?"

"I guess so," the VP would say, rolling his eyes.

After about the tenth meeting that went like this, Mary explained her theory behind all those questions. "I know I sound like an idiot, but the truth is that [the VP] doesn't have a clue about how much work it takes to get these things done. And most of the time, the people who should be speaking up don't ask enough questions so they waste time doing a lot of work that's not necessary," she said.

She was right, of course. Ultimately, by allowing herself to appear somewhat dense, Mary used

Multi-Asking to help the group gain clarity, organize our workflow, and make the most of our limited resources.

Your Team, Your Rules

Another way being a member of a team can help you achieve success is that teams that deliver consistently tend to be rewarded. One woman I know, we'll call her Carol, carefully built and tended to her team over a period of years, starting when she joined her company as a director. The company was floundering a bit, falling just short of the degree of success that upper management was demanding.

Carol took a look around and realized that part of the problem was that there were invisible but oh-so-sturdy walls separating departments, walls that made it almost impossible to get anything done. The head of one group didn't like the head of another group, so he actively discouraged his staff from providing information that the other group needed. In response, the other group operated with a mindset that went something like this: "If they aren't going to help us, we're going to undermine them." And this kind of thing was rampant throughout the organization.

Carol realized that she probably couldn't change that; the only way to fix this mess was to build a team that would work around those invisible walls.

Obvious members of her team included the people who reported to her, but Carol also developed powerful relationships with people in other departments by applying what can only be called "guerrilla tactics" to getting things done. She never sent emails requesting assistance, nor did she call a lot of meetings. When she needed data for a report, she'd figure out which member of her team could get that data and, dropping by their office just to say "hello," she'd ask them for it. And she encouraged her direct reports to do the same. "Don't play the game by the established rules," she said. "Play the game so we can win."

One thing to note is that Carol understood that the *we* who could win included everyone in the company, not just her team. "I always figured that our company should be trying to outmaneuver the competition, not each other," she explained. Radical, eh?

By building a team, Carol was able to break through those invisible walls, creating opportunities to streamline processes and make things happen. In other words, Carol didn't play by the rules that had stopped her company from reaching certain goals. As a result, within a year sales were up and Carol was promoted to vice president of her department. And her team rose with her. Obviously her direct reports moved up—a manager moved into the director position, someone else moved into the manager role, and so on—but what was really interesting was that team members in other departments moved up, too. In fact, that department head who discouraged cooperation left the company "to explore other opportunities," and Carol's team member in that department took his place.

Oh sure, there were some catty coworkers who claimed that these rewards were the result of "kissing up to Carol." But in reality, by playing by its own rules, the team Carol created actually delivered.

Your Inner Bitch would like to remind you that you don't have to deal with every irritant that comes your way during the day. But never choose silence when an issue really matters, or silence will lead you down the path to Toxic Niceness.

Chapter Five
Pick Your Battles

Your Inner Bitch is practically custom-made for dealing with the inevitable conflicts that arise in our professional lives. And she is even better equipped for figuring out how to resolve those issues. Being in touch with your Inner Bitch means that you'll not only survive the days when the office feels like a battlefield, you'll learn what makes you thrive in spite of the often-ridiculous skirmishes involved in office politics without resorting to such non-Bitchy behaviors as nastiness, quavering in the face of authority, and magical thinking about the day when you'll feel powerful enough to act on your own (or someone else's) behalf.

Let's explore some of the typical conflicts the Inner Bitch will help you deal with.

Catch-22

My friend Minnie ran into this catch-22 situation shortly after she was promoted to a managerial position in a company where she had worked for years. Part of the reason she had been boosted into the new job was the sudden departure of the former manager, who had "left to pursue other interests," which is, of course, code for being fired. In this case, the axe had fallen because someone finally figured out that this guy had been telling his team to ignore certain directives issued from on high. "Those idiots don't now what they're doing," he'd say. "We'll do things my way." The results of doing things his way included a database that didn't function properly, causing missed deadlines and—most damaging—a drop in revenue because the company couldn't deliver their products efficiently. Minnie inherited what some would call "a mess," but she rolled up her sleeves and waded in to figure out how to fix it.

Another reason for some Inner Bitch outrage:

According to a study by Catalyst, a research and advisory organization, the male-held stereotype that woman are poor problem-solvers creates a catch-22 situation. Because of the stereotype, people are reluctant to follow the directions of women leaders, and, with their problem-solving skills undermined, women lose interpersonal power.*

* Women "Take Care," Men "Take Charge": Stereotyping of U.S. Business Leaders Exposed. A 2005 study from the Catalyst website: catalystwomen.com.

Pretty quickly she realized that the first thing required was rebuilding the database from the ground up, so she got her team together and laid out what she thought needed to happen. But because databases weren't her area of expertise, she missed a couple of necessary steps, which one man, Joe, seemed to take great pleasure in pointing out before declaring, "it can't be done. We'll have to come up with work-arounds." The rest of the team all nodded in agreement with this assessment, which rattled Minnie no end.

"Why can't it be done?" she asked.

The answer consisted of a lot of technical jargon that Minnie not only didn't understand, but that gave her a headache. She ended the meeting, walked into her office, shut the door, dimmed the lights, and laid her head down on her desk.

"I just knew I'd failed," she told me when recounting this story. But then something magical happened. Mistaking the signals sent forth by Minnie's closed door and darkened office, Joe made what can only be called an error in judgment.

Standing in the hallway, surrounded by the team, Joe gloated that this was the end of Minnie. "That idiot doesn't know what she's doing," he said.

One of the other guys pointed out that the database really did need to be completely over-hauled and that doing so was actually possible, to which Joe replied, "Well, you know that, and I know that, but she doesn't, and who wants to work that hard? No, we'll just do things my way until we get rid of the bitch."

"That's when my Inner Bitch took over," Minnie told me. She stood up, opened her door and said, "Hello, boys. Perhaps I wasn't clear—my job is to set the agenda, yours is to make it happen. So you," she pointed to the guy who had said overhauling the database was possible, "are in charge of developing a step-by-step plan. I want a draft of that by the end of day tomorrow, and you," she pointed at Joe, "can come into my office."

The group scattered, and Minnie shut the door again as Joe sat down. "Are you going to fire me now?" he asked.

"No, I'm going to explain some simple economics to you. We don't fix this, the company keeps losing money. The company keeps losing money, and we don't have jobs, so I won't have to fire you. But if you ever try to play that game with me again, I will. Clear?"

"Crystal," Joe said.

"Now I'm sure that Jerry could use some help in developing that plan, so why don't you go give him a hand?"

When I asked her what happened next, Minnie told me that Jerry and Joe delivered the plan to her the next morning and that for the next two months everyone on the team worked days, nights, and weekends to rebuild the database. "Funny thing is that Joe worked the hardest of all," she said. "And if anybody complained about the amount of work, he'd explain some simple economics to them."

The most important lesson that Minnie learned, however, was this: when you are the boss, you are the bitch, and if you're going to have the name, you might as well play the game your way. Being in touch with your Inner Bitch means you're not afraid to make the rules.

A Higher Authority

There will be times when someone else is making the rules—sometimes it will be your immediate boss, sometimes it will be someone much higher up the food chain than you. So what do you do when you disagree with what that person has asked you to do? Your Inner Bitch wants you to make your point concisely, thank her for listening, and then stop talking. Knowing when to end the conversation isn't Toxic Niceness, that's smart business. Another option would be a judicious "I'll think about that."

One woman I know, Linda, used this technique to brilliant effect. Linda was standing in her boss's office when a senior vice president of another department came in to say that some information her assistant had promised Linda for a time-sensitive report wouldn't be ready in time. "So here's what I was thinking," the SVP said, "We'll get you the raw data, and if you have any questions, you can touch base with each individual in my group to get an answer."

"I don't know if I can get the report done in time that way, but let me think about how I can make that work," Linda said.

"Or we could give you the raw data, and you

could come up with a list of questions and we could answer them all at once," the SVP suggested.

"Okay, let me think about those ideas," Linda said again.

"Or we could try to put the data together in a sort of organized way, get that to you, and go from there." This was exactly what had been promised in the first place, so Linda agreed that would be a great approach. When the SVP left, Linda's boss started to laugh.

"You know, if you'd resisted at all, she would have just had them give you the raw data," he said. "Then what would you have done?"

"Lucky for me, I don't have to think about that," Linda said.

Picking Your Battles

When we suffer from Toxic Niceness, we believe in somedays, as in "Some day I'll feel powerful enough to speak my mind about the things that bother me," or "Some day I'll have the corner office, and then they'll have to listen to me."

Does the Inner Bitch have to wait to speak her mind until we've attained some level of power in the workplace? I don't think so. Being in touch with our Inner Bitch will empower us today, no matter what level of position we hold.

For instance, my Inner Bitch came in handy one day when I was working at a law firm. (Is it any wonder I eventually changed professions?) The physical setups of most law firms—and most corporate offices, in fact—is worthy of a full-blown sociological study. The attorneys (and in corporate offices, directors, some managers) have offices on the outside of the building, with windows and doors. Secretaries and cubicle workers are in glorified hallways. At this particular law firm I shared an alcove with Carol, another secretary, with our cubicles separated from the hall by four-foot-tall barriers. The effect was of working in a kind of fishbowl: we couldn't make a phone call without any passerby being able to hear every word; we couldn't have a private conversation; being able to focus required the metaphoric equivalent of blinders and earplugs; and if the door to an attorney's office was open we were privy to every utterance.

One day I was working on a fairly large project that required considerable concentration, when one of the younger attorneys—I'll call him Sam—got a phone call that started off as a discussion about some business matter. However, at some point, the conversation took a more personal tone, and the topic seemed to be some woman the client was dating.

"So, she's hot?" Sam queried. Carol and I exchanged glances punctuated by raised eyebrows. She shook her head. "Yeah, but have you seen her in a bathing suit? They can hide an awful lot with the right underpinnings, you know."

I stood up, crossed the hall and closed his office door.

"Oh, man, he's not going to like that," Carol said.

"Probably not," I replied, turning back to my computer screen.

A few minutes later, Sam's door opened. He called me into his office, and asked me to take a seat. "What was that about?" he asked, closing the door.

"I don't feel like I need to hear conversations like the one you were having," I said.

"Maybe you don't get it, I'm a lawyer. I can have any kind of conversation I want," he said.

"Yep, you sure can. But I don't need to have them imposed on me," I said, getting up from the chair and opening the door. "Having to listen to conversations about the relative hotness of your client's girlfriend makes me uncomfortable, so I closed your door. If you have a problem with that, maybe we should go talk to the senior partner. I'm sure he has an opinion on how appropriate my behavior was, and I'm sure he's heard the phrase 'hostile work environment.'" Steve just stared at me. "Yeah, that's what I thought. I'm going back to work now."

When I sat down again, there was a note from Carol on my desk. "I've been wanting to do something like that for years," it read.

"Why haven't you?" I asked Carol, holding up her note.

"I'm just a secretary," she shrugged.

Your Inner Bitch knows, however, that without the support staffs of the world—you know, those who are "just" secretaries—nothing would ever get done. This adds up to some substantial power, when you think about it. She also knows that there's a name for not speaking up about the things that bother us: Toxic Niceness.

Taking Care of Business, Inner Bitch Style:

When you make a mistake at work, and you will, your Inner Bitch wants you to remember what Rosalind Russell once said, "Flops are a part of life's menu, and I've never been a girl to miss out on any of the courses."

Chapter Six
Errors in Judgment, or, The Big Oops!

*B*etter yet, your Inner Bitch will help you deal with mistakes. Mistakes are inevitable, after all, because as someone once said: To err is human.

"Oh, no! Was that my 'out-loud' voice?"

Inevitably, you will have an "Oh, shit!" moment at work. When it happens, your Inner Bitch wants you to take a deep breath and move through it. No matter how fervently you want the floor to open up so you can magically disappear, the odds are against that actually happening.

Once upon a time I worked as the receptionist at a law firm. Although being a receptionist would seem to be a fairly straight-forward job—answer the phone, greet clients when they walk in the door, tidy up the reception area—in reality it's more akin to being on the front lines of an ongoing battle of wills. I had to keep track of which clients got ushered into offices immediately, who was to be kept cooling their heels, which deal was hot, which opposing counsel was perpetually relegated to "take a message" status. It was exhausting.

Most challenging, however, was one of my favorite attorneys—I'll call him Mickey. Mickey was a charmer in that "gotta love that naughty boy" way. He was also a senior partner and a big rainmaker. Mickey brought so much money into the firm that his naughty-boy behavior was tolerated from the top down. How he got any work done was mysterious, because Mickey spent a good portion of his days roaming through the office chatting with the secretaries, getting a cup of coffee, and "conferring" with his colleagues on such legal matters as the best place to get lunch that day. Primary on his daily "to do" list, however, was avoiding phone calls. Mickey hated taking phone calls. When client called for him, I would put them on hold and hit Mickey's office line. "Whaaaaat?" he wailed.

"Mr. Bigshot's on the phone for you."

"Damn it, I don't wanna talk to that imbecile," he'd moan. "Tell him I died. Tell him I've been buried under an avalanche of paperwork related to his stupid deal. Tell him I've run off to Tahiti to emulate Gaugin."

"I'll put him through to your secretary," I'd say.

When his wife called, it was even worse, and

she called at least six times a day.

This went on for weeks. Every time I'd call him, Mickey would let loose with strings of epithets, bemoaning his lot in life and chastising me for bothering him. I'd either take a message or put the call through to Mickey's secretary, whose primary skill seemed to be tolerating Mickey. But one day the phones were ringing nonstop, and every single call was vital. In the midst of all of this, one of Mickey's clients called. "Elizabeth, I absolutely need to speak to Mickey," he said.

"Hold, please," I replied, putting him on hold and hitting Mickey's button. Mickey was in rare form that day, because his secretary was out sick and he actually had some work to do for the client who was calling.

"That bastard, I wouldn't be up against the wall like this if it wasn't for him. I don't want to talk to him, he's nothing but trouble. Tell him I. . . ."

As Mickey started winding up for a prolonged

diatribe, two other lines started to ring. "Hey!" I snapped. "My job here is to answer the phone and put the calls through, for which I'm paid substantially less than you. Now, I've got two other lines ringing, and I'm sure that whoever is calling expects someone to actually answer. Do you want to take this call or should I take a message?"

After a moment of silence, Mickey told me to put the call through. I hit the right button, took the other two calls, and wondered where exactly I'd put my resume. Suddenly Mickey was standing in front of me with his hands in his pockets. "Helloooo," I said, hoping to stall the axe from falling.

"You know, nobody talks to me like that," Mickey said.

"Mmmhmmm," I replied, because I was pretty sure he was about to fire me in some spectacular way, and most of my energy was focused on my fervent desire for the floor to open up and swallow me whole.

"Not even my mother talks to me like that," he said.

"Huh," I managed.

"Which I guess explains why I'm such a brat. I'm sorry if I've made your job difficult. I'll try to remember to be a little more courteous, okay?"

"Um, okay," I said.

"Okay," he nodded and walked out of the reception area. From that moment on, Mickey was unerringly courteous to me. He still only took phone calls under duress, but the tirades stopped. And he started stopping by with little treats for me during the day—a cup of coffee in the morning, some chocolate in the afternoon. We'd chat a bit, and one day he asked me if I was happy being a receptionist.

"Well, I don't mind it, but I'm getting a little bored," I said.

"And a little more money wouldn't hurt, would it?" he said.

"It sure wouldn't."

Within two weeks I was promoted to a secretarial position, which paid a lot better than the receptionist job. And Mickey became my mentor, helping me decide that I needed to move on when it became clear that I'd run out of opportunities at that firm and helping me get another higher-paid position. So, in that case, what seemed like a mistake turned out to be a good move.

There are, however, times when a mistake is just a mistake.

The Big Booboo

Some mistakes are clerical in nature, such as the time Gloria conducted what can only be referred to as a full-fledged marketing campaign to find a new job. She carefully researched companies all over the country to find those that interested her, designed a four-color presentation promoting "the product known as Gloria" on which she spent a small fortune having bound copies printed, and set up her dining room as her base of operations. Rather than use anything as pedestrian as envelopes and regular mail, Gloria put her presentation in linen-covered boxes, which were to be shipped by overnight delivery. Naturally, many of her friends were pressed into service, so I dropped by to assist her with one day's delivery.

"The presentation goes in first, then my resume. The cover letter goes on top," Gloria instructed.

As I put together my first package, something odd caught my eye. I picked up the copy of Gloria's resume to get a better look and, sure enough, there was a typo. "Hey, Gloria, where did you go to college?" I asked.

"Yale," she replied.

"Yale, Y-A-L-E or Yale, Y-E-A-L?"

"Y-A-L . . . oh, my gawd!" She snatched the resume out of my hands, her mouth open in a silent scream. Because right there in black and white was evidence that Gloria had not graduated summa cum laude from a notable Ivy League school but had, in fact, gotten her degree from the lesser-known Yeal University—which she'd bragged about to some one hundred companies across the U.S.

We laugh about it now, because it turns out that very few people caught the mistake, and Gloria got a number of job offers as a result of her campaign. But when she's grousing about some mistake one of her direct reports has made, I always ask Gloria how much she's donated to the Yeal alumni fund this year.

Some mistakes, however, can only be filed under "L" for "lethal," because you can never recover from having made them.

My friend Barbara is what I'd call a Big Wheel.

She's got a big corner office, numerous direct reports (and indirect reports), plus an assistant who keeps track of her schedule, books her travel plans, fields her phone calls, and who has—this completely blows my mind—an assistant. Yep, Barb is so important her *assistant* has an assistant. Big. Wheel. So one would imagine that her rise through the ranks of the corporate world has been singularly lacking in missteps. One would be wrong. Barb's had her share of "oh shit" moments, including but what she calls "The Big Mother Booboo."

Right around the time Barb was recruited for her current job, she was also being courted by another company—one for which she'd always wanted to work. She maneuvered her way through the first and second rounds of discussions with this company (at Barb's level one doesn't interview, one has "discussions" wherein all parties get a feel for whether or not the candidate is a good fit, and vice versa), and she was on her way to headquarters for her first meeting with the CEO and president. Just as Barb was getting off the highway, this guy on a motorcycle got behind her, riding her tail and flashing his headlight at her. Because there was no way for her to get out of his way at that point, she raised one hand off the steering wheel in a sort of "what?" gesture, which elicited a long blast of his horn. So Barb sped up a little, and as soon as she could she moved over to let him pass, at which point she rolled down her window, made another, universally understood gesture at him and yelled an epithet at him as he roared by.

Yes, of course the guy on the motorcycle was the CEO she was about to meet with. And, yes, of course, he recognized her. Although Barb offered him what she thought was an effective, light-hearted apology, she didn't get hired. "I really wanted that job, too," she still moans when she tells this story. The worst part is that she frequently sees this guy at industry functions, and every time he reminds her of her lapse into road rage. Of course, I try to tell her that anyone who didn't understand her side of that incident probably wouldn't be someone she wanted to work with, but Barb still regrets the whole thing.

Turning It Around

I've always believed that we learn more from our mistakes than from our successes, in part because we think more about the errors we make. After all, have you ever lain awake all night replaying some triumph? No, we usually reserve bouts of insomnia for reviewing some gaffe we've made—like the nightmare job interview or that time in first grade when . . . well, you remember.

So how does the Inner Bitch handle a mistake? Let me think about that.

Grace under Fire

Mistakes, obviously, are going to happen, and your Inner Bitch wants you to deal with them immediately. There's nothing to be gained (and a lot to lose) by pretending that, as I once did, you forgot to add in an entire month's expenditures when you were coming up with next year's budget. In a situation like this, it's imperative that you run the numbers again and issue a revision as quickly—and gracefully—as possible.

Let's Face It

What if you're not the first one to realize that you made a blunder? Chances are, someone (usually your boss) is going to come looking for you, and it won't be pretty. For example, as managing editor for a weekly newspaper, I once sent the cover to press with a misspelled word in the main headline. When the first stack of papers arrived on the editor-in-chief's desk, she let out a shout of disbelief and then charged out into the production area waving the offending document. "I should fire you right now!" she hollered at me as my coworkers took a sudden interest in the contents of their lowest desk drawers. Although at that moment I wished a tornado would sweep me away to Oz, my only real option was to issue a quick apology, which did nothing to stop the tidal wave of abuse from my boss. Fortunately, she had to take a breath at some point, which is when I said, "Listen, I admit this is a major f*#&-up, but can we at least do this in your office?"

"No!" she shouted, then continued her tirade.

It wasn't the best moment in my career. The best thing I can say about it is that I didn't get canned. However, it was the moment I realized that it was time for me to move on. Not only because my boss was abusive (and not just to me), but also because making a mistake like that was a sure sign that I'd lost interest in the job itself. My Front Page BooBoo spurred me into action; I did a job search and ended up with a position that paid better and had the added benefit of getting me away from that abusive boss.

"Fall Seven Times, Get Up Eight"

Your Inner Bitch really appreciates this venerable bit of wisdom, because it reminds us that we can overcome anything as long as we're willing to pick ourselves up, dust ourselves off, and start all over again.

Apply the 10-Year Rule

Chances are, even what seems like the Worst Mistake Ever isn't really the worst mistake in the history of the world. Think of all the competition there is for that [dis]honor, like the fashion known as hot pants, the Le Car, or the most recent superstar marital scandal. In reality, with the passage of time most mistakes simply fade into the woodwork, and no one remembers them but you. Your Inner Bitch wants you to remember that in ten years (or five, or two, or even a few months), the mistake that seems major at the moment will have transformed itself into a little speed bump on the road to success. And, as Rosalind Russell once said, "Flops are a part of life's menu, and I've never been a girl to miss out on any of the courses."

Of course, there are some mistakes we should go out of our way to avoid.

Mistakes You Can't Overcome

There are some errors that are career death. For instance

❋ Sleeping with the boss: This is never a good idea. Although some might see this as a way to curry favor, as Ellen Goodman once pointedly asked, "If women can sleep their way to the top, how come they aren't there? There must be an epidemic of insomnia out there." The simple truth is that one (or both) of you will lose your job. Imagine trying to explain the reason you were let go at your next interview.

✻ Idle threats: Making statements such as, "If you don't give me a raise, I'm leaving," isn't good business, and it won't make most bosses budge during a salary negotiation.

✻ Unethical behavior: Chances are you'll never overcome a public disclosure that you were the one who ordered an extra shredder to get rid of evidence of corporate malfeasance (whether you were responsible for the malfeasance in the first place or you were just covering for someone else). Even if you do manage to get hired someplace else, the shadow cast by this kind of misjudgment is sure to be a long one. Your Inner Bitch knows that if something doesn't feel right, it probably isn't right—so just say no to that kind of thing. You may lose your job, but you'll be able to look yourself in the mirror.

"What would life be if we had no courage to attempt anything?"
—Vincent Van Gogh

Chapter Seven
Thinking about Making Things Happen

*A*n almost daily challenge we face in the workplace is other people's lassitude. What does your Inner Bitch do when the folks you work with can't seem to get out of their own way?

One friend of mine has figured out a brilliant way for getting around office politics—instead of asking for permission, she would rather ask for forgiveness (although she rarely has to). Jeannie works for a nonprofit that relies on donations and fund-raisers; one of her job duties is coming up with ways to promote the organization.

"The 'leadership' at my job pretty much avoids ever making any kind of decision," she explained. "When I first started working there, I'd toss out ideas about things I wanted to do to make us more visible, and everyone would sort of hem and haw. No one ever came right out and said no, but they never said yes, either. So nothing much ever happened because, as an organization, we couldn't get out of our own way."

The turning point for Jeannie came, as these things often do, during a chance encounter at an industry function. "I was talking to someone who works at a big talent agency and mentioned that I was thinking about asking one of the agency's clients—not one of the big celebrities, but some-one who was kind of well-known—to act as an honorary chair for an event we were hoping to put together. She gave me her card and told me to call her the next day because she was having a meeting with that person to discuss how they could pump up his image."

When Jeannie called, the agent said the celebrity was thrilled about the idea. The only problem was that he was going to be shooting a movie on location halfway around the world, and he was leaving in two months. "What can we do before then?" the agent asked.

"Let me think about that, and I'll call you back," Jeannie replied. Then she called the director of a local theater and asked if there were any events coming up that could be turned into a fund-raiser. "We just had another celebrity back out of a commitment to narrate the holiday show, so we're scrambling."

"Have I got a replacement for you!" Jeannie said. She got all the details and called back the agent; the agent called the celebrity, who said he would be delighted. Then Jeannie went into the weekly staff meeting and announced what she'd made happen. Everyone was thrilled, and the fund-raiser ended up surpassing the nonprofit's goal for donations by an enormous amount.

"We had to do a lot of running around to get press releases sent out and alert our usual donors, but that's what email is for," Jeannie said. "Ever since then I stopped waiting for the higher-ups to sign off on my ideas, I just do the legwork to get things going, then report what I've done."

Of course, there are some places where that wouldn't work at all, but your Inner Bitch knows that there are a lot of detours around organizational speed bumps.

Speed Bump Detours

By their very nature, speed bumps are designed to slow you down. This might be a useful technique for controlling drivers, but it's counterproductive in the workplace. Your Inner Bitch wants you to forge ahead—or, better yet, find a way around the obstacles that lie in wait on the road to success.

Playing to the Bottom Line

For instance, my friend Ellen is in charge of her company's website. "No one really understands what it takes to make the website work, so what I do is completely mysterious to them," she said. "I used to try to explain things to them, but their eyes would glaze over seconds into my little spiels. They zoned out so completely that they never even heard what the end results of what I was doing with the site would be."

That didn't mean the decision makers at her company had no opinions about what she was doing, however. They actually had plenty of those, plus a lot of ideas about improving the site—many of which she had just finished telling them were already in the works. The problem was that none of those ideas were actually feasible with the budget she had been given, and because they didn't understand what it took to implement new designs, they told her to work within the existing budget.

She finally realized that no one cared about the details; they just cared about the outcome. So she began pitching her ideas from the bottom line up. "You know how we may be able to increase revenues by 10 percent? I could do this with the website." This tactic certainly got their attention. Then she would add something such as, "Making that happen would only take another $X; can we find that somewhere?"

The Naysayer

Once upon a time I worked with someone who said no to every new idea anyone had. When I was fresh on that job, I spent the better part of my first month coming up with a new process for tracking production in our department, a project that involved sitting down with everyone to determine the bottlenecks that were keeping us from working together efficiently. Everyone warned me that whatever I came up with was going to be shot down in the end, but I didn't listen. After all, this was one of the reasons I'd been hired. So I put together a nifty little presentation with charts and all sorts of figures, set up a meeting with my boss, and showed him my plan.

"Oh, no, that's never going to work," he said. "You'll never get everyone to buy into this."

"Well, everyone I've talked to is very enthusiastic," I told him.

"I don't think so," he responded, ending the meeting right then and there.

I was . . . well, "annoyed" doesn't come close to describing how I felt. "Stymied" comes to mind, as do the phrases undermined, negated, and royally ticked off. After all, I'd spent a lot of time on developing this plan; to have it dismissed out of hand was maddening. Naturally, I told one of my coworkers what had happened, because a girl's gotta vent.

"I warned you, but what are you going to do?" he shrugged.

"I'll think about that," I said. Then I started implementing the changes I could within my own group. I cut out some processes I'd identified as superfluous and instituted some new ways of doing things. Within a couple of weeks, my group was exceeding its target deadlines substantially. None of the other groups in the department changed anything, so all the bottlenecks were now in their court, so to speak.

A month later, our boss called all the managers into an emergency meeting (this guy loved meetings!), and he came armed with a big old chart he'd had his assistant make. "Look at this! The editorial group is way ahead of the rest of you.

We've got to get more efficient!" Then he proceeded to outline the very plan he'd shot down when I presented it to him. When I pointed that out to him after the meeting, he looked at me as if I had two heads. "No it's not, it's completely different. Your plan had everything starting from here," he pointed to an action item on his timeline, then ran his finger back down the chart. "Mine starts here."

"Yes, I see that you've added a planning meeting I didn't have, but the rest of it is my plan," I said.

"No, it's not. I spent a lot of time developing this whole thing from the ground up. Now I have to go show this to my boss," he replied, waving "his" plan as he walked down the hall. The worst part was that he actually had talked himself into believing that this was true.

That was when I figured out that the only way around his automatic "no" was to make sure he thought that any new ideas were actually his—and I also had to figure out how to make sure other people in the company knew that wasn't necessarily the case. Dicey, eh? You bet it was. So I called my outside team together for a little whine and cheese party and asked for their advice.

"This is so unfair!" I whined.

"Yes it is, sweetie," they all concurred. "Pass the cheese, please, and we should open another bottle of wine while we think about what to do."

I've forgotten some of what transpired at that meeting (for obvious reasons), but the solution we ended up with was simply brilliant. Whenever I wanted to get him to agree to something new, I was to simply plant the seed with a simple, "Don't you think we could? . . ." When he responded with the inevitable "No," I would just agree with him. The key to making sure that I got credit for the idea was this: just before going into our meeting, I was to send him an email with the suggestion and copy anyone else to whom my idea might matter. Since my boss was notorious for rarely even looking at emails from anyone who reported to him, this plan bordered on genius.

I had an opportunity to try it out the very next day when the managers (including me) all got together to discuss how to deal with an upcoming rush period. I had an idea—hey, that's what they were paying me for!—and he told me all the reasons it wouldn't work. But I had sent the suggested email to a fairly long list of other people. The pay-off came during a company-wide strategy meeting about a week later. At some point, my boss started off in his usual way, "I was thinking about this and came up with an idea; what if we? . . ."

People all around the conference table looked from him to me and back again, then all eyes turned to Jake, the president of the company, who said, "Gee, Henry, that *is* a good idea. I even

thought that was a great idea when Elizabeth suggested it in her email last week."

Your Inner Bitch wants you to remember that your most valuable hours aren't necessarily those you spend at work.

Chapter Eight
Time Off for Good Behavior

Your Inner Bitch knows that you have to work, but she also knows that you have a life. If you don't have a life away from work, well, your Inner Bitch wants you to make one.

Taking Care of Business, Inner Bitch Style:
The power to actually take your vacation days belongs to you. Your Inner Bitch wants you to use that power instead of rolling off those days you've earned into yet another year.

Time Off for Good Behavior

Your Inner Bitch knows that vacations are essential for a number of reasons:

1. You're not at work.
2. Ideally, you are indulging yourself in ways you wouldn't in your everyday life, such as sleeping late or having daily massages or spending an entire day reading (or writing) a novel. Oh, and maybe even trying something like parasailing.
3. Spending time away from the pressures of work allows you to create memories.
4. Travel can expand your mind, providing you with new ideas about how you really want to live.

For example, my friend Nancy went on vacation and came home with a whole new life. Really. After years of not taking time off from work, she decided to join some friends for a ski trip to the French Alps. (Talk about saving up for something special!) On that trip she learned how to ski (in the French Alps), tried snowshoeing for the first time, and met the man she ended up marrying.

The irony is that she almost canceled her trip because of a potential problem at work. A week before she was scheduled to leave, a last-minute project was suddenly dumped on her team. Even though she developed a plan for dealing with the extra work, Nancy was pretty sure that the project would be a disaster unless she was there to make sure everything went smoothly. "I can't go," she told me.

"Let's think about this," I replied, and then proceeded to list her concerns. "You've made a plan, right? Your team is a professional bunch who are experts at their assigned tasks, right? And there's nothing specific you have to do to make this project happen; the only thing you'd do is oversee the whole thing?"

"Right, right, and yes," Nancy said.

"You're going," I told her.

"But, but, but," Nancy protested, citing numerous work-related reasons why it was impossible for her to go on vacation. The more she talked, the clearer it became that she'd gotten so wrapped up in work that she couldn't imagine not being there. This became so clear, in fact, that even Nancy realized that she *really* needed a vacation. Even better, she realized that she had fallen into one of the traps of Toxic Success: she was very successful at work, but the rest of her life was in a shambles. "I've got to get a life," she concluded. Then she went home and packed her bags.

Of course, not all of us can jet off to Europe (or even take a road trip to Cousin Etta's house in the suburbs). But your Inner Bitch still wants you to make the most of your vacation time. In all truthfulness, one of the best vacations I ever had was spent organizing every drawer, closet, and bookcase in my house. After a day of sifting through my belongings, deciding what I wanted to keep and what to get rid of, I certainly didn't want to make dinner and spend the evening watching TV, so I went out for dinner with friends every night. By the time I went back to the office, my house was in order, and I'd had some wonderful time with the people who matter to me most. It wasn't the showiest vacation I'd ever had—no one wanted to see pictures of my alphabetized bookshelves—but it left me energized in a way I never would have expected and ready to do my life.

Doing Life

The cold hard fact is that most of us have only five hours in every day to devote to our "real" lives. Five hours. Does that sound right? Let's think about that by breaking an average day into what we'll call *action items:*

* Preparation action: Wake up. Conduct your morning rituals—drink coffee (or whatever), shower, dress, grab a foil-wrapped breakfast pastry, and go. This can take anywhere from ten minutes to two hours, depending on your individual circumstances. For instance, some people claim they actually make real food for breakfast and sit down to eat it while reading the paper. Some people work out in the morning (bless their hearts). Other people have children, which adds a certain drag time to the whole preparation extravaganza.

* Commuting action: This can take anywhere from five minutes (no, really, I had a friend

who lived across the street from his office for a while) to a few hours. One friend of mine commutes nearly three hours *each way* to her job, but she has negotiated a schedule that lets her work at home two days a week most of the time.

- Working action: Most jobs require that you participate in them for at least eight hours each work day, although that is broken up by the magical event we call lunch.
- Lunch-hour action: Yep, an entire sixty-minute block of time during which you can meet a friend for a meal, go shopping, meditate, go to the gym . . . unless you work in one of those places that gives you a half-hour lunch (and your Inner Bitch has some thoughts about that).
- Sleep action: The recommended daily minimum is eight hours, but how is anyone supposed to catch their favorite late night talk show

or get a little quality time (by which I mean, of course, sex or reading or what have you).

What's missing? Oh, right. Real-life action, which includes (but is not limited to) laundry, the procurement and preparation of foodstuffs, helping the kids with their homework, watching TV, performing basic home maintenance, talking with friends, and actually having relationships with your lover/partner/husband, your children, your pets—you know, *everything* that is *not work*.

So, how do you fit a whole life into five measly hours every day? Let's think about that.

Multitasking

Your Inner Bitch knows that women are specialists in the art of multitasking. If you doubt this for one minute, call a woman friend on the average evening and ask her what she's doing. "Oh, nothing," she'll probably say. "I'm just finishing cleaning up the kitchen, and I've got the bath going for the kids . . . hold on, I just have to put this load of laundry in the dryer . . . no, Plum, you add the eggs after the cake mix, here, I'll turn on the oven . . . what? No, I wasn't talking to you, honey; I'm on the phone with Loretta. Sorry, Loretta. What's going on with that situation at work? I was thinking about that the other day, and what I would do is. . . ."

"Nothing," in this case, equals six things. All at the same time. Sounds crazy when it's put down in black and white, but let's think about it—what do you get done in an average half-hour in the evening? If someone were making a movie of your typical day, there would probably be count-less examples of you multitasking without even thinking about it. The truth is, stuff has to get done, and we're usually the ones who do it. If not, we're the ones who are making sure it happens.

Is this a bad thing? I don't think so, as long as we make our innate talent for multitasking really work for us. And, obviously, your Inner Bitch wants you to make sure that it does, because if multitasking is only working for the other people in our lives, that's a sure sign that Toxic Niceness is rearing its ugly head.

How does the Inner Bitch multitask? With great aplomb, naturally. Here are some examples, as reported by actual women in touch with their Inner Bitches:

* Drive-time entertainment: During the commute to work, my friend Linda catches up on her reading (she takes public transportation—if you drive, listen to audiobooks) or enjoys a phone call with another commuting friend. This is not a time for making business-related phone calls, unless there is a crisis at work (although if she happens to be in the midst of the mother of all traffic jams, she does alert the office).

* Maximum lunch: Once a week, my friend

Jeannine does what she calls a "power shop." She goes to the megamart near her office and gets most of the groceries and related items she needs. Meats, dairy, and frozen stuff get packed into a giant cooler with ice packs, on top of which she puts her produce. Naturally, this takes a little planning, and it doesn't work during the hottest months of the year, but this saves Jeannine from having to spend part of her weekend shopping for food. My friends Sue and Ann have a slight variation on this: they have dinner together then go grocery shopping every Friday night, which gives them an opportunity to socialize with one another and get a necessary job done, without their husbands and kids around (because who wants to go grocery shopping?).

✽ Me time: Most of the evening's tasks are taken care of: dinner is done; the kids are in bed; and the dog has been walked. While enjoying her favorite TV program, my friend Claudia gets some laundry folded, rides her stationary bike (or the elliptical or just does some crunches) for half an hour, then does her nails. The well-known side benefit of doing one's nails is that this forces us to do absolutely nothing while the polish dries, which means an opportunity to actually relax. This brings us to an interesting point, to wit: "Remember, you're a human being, not a human doing." Your Inner Bitch wants you to stop the insanity of trying to accomplish too much in a single day.

And in the End. . . . . .

Your Inner Bitch knows that what ultimately matters will not be how much your coworkers like you; it will not be how high you climb on the corporate ladder; and it will not be the money you earn (even though all of these things certainly have value). To ensure that you have a life worth living, your Inner Bitch wants to remind you that there's a lot of truth to that old saying, "No one on their deathbed says, 'I wish I'd spent more time at work.'" The real reason it's vital to figure out how to create a work-life balance is that it will save you from Toxic Success.

Think about that.

"Money is the medium of exchange, and it's how you make things happen. To say you hate it is some far-fetched, idealistic crap."

—Bobby Seale

Chapter Nine
"Bitch" Rhymes with "Rich"

*S*tudy after study shows that unlike men, women don't ask for the salary they want, they don't ask for well-deserved raises, and they hardly ever negotiate for more than is offered to them. The bottom line is that as a result, over the course of her career the average woman leaves more than half a million dollars on the table (and available to be put into someone else's pocket).

Half a million dollars. That's $500,000.

Honey, that's a lot of money. If you have a career that lasts twenty years, that's $25,000 a year you're missing out on.

So what stops us from asking for every red cent we deserve? Once again, Toxic Niceness is probably to blame. Of course, there are some other issues involved.

For example, even though the Equal Pay Act was passed in 1963, in 2004 full-time working women were paid 76¢ for every dollar received by men. When the act was passed, women got 59¢ on the dollar. In other words, the wage gap has narrowed by less than half a penny per year.

Part of the problem, however, has got to be that those of us who suffer from Toxic Niceness are settling for less because, in part, Nice Girls don't ask for what they need. I've said it before and I'll say it again: Work is what we do for money. Money in this society equals power. When we suffer from Toxic Niceness, we fear power. We think it's unattractive. We may couch this belief in phrases like "money's just not important to me," but it's really that we fear power.

That's just silly. Is power important? Of course it is. Is money important? Well, sure it is, and not just because it represents buying power and because being able to pay our bills beats not being able to pay our bills any day. No, money is also important because, as the great philosopher Coco Chanel once said, "Money for me has only one sound: Liberty."

Think about it. If you had that extra $25,000 a year, you might end up socking at least some of it away in what I like to call a "Liberty Fund." A Liberty Fund would provide a financial cushion just in case you wanted to do something really outrageous, such as start your own business or buy that little villa in Italy you've always dreamed of having. By not doing everything we can to get the money we deserve, we do a lot to cheat ourselves out of attaining our dreams. And all because Toxic Niceness makes us think that caring about money (and power) is unattractive.

In other words, Toxic Niceness is hazardous to our well-being, and it's hazardous to your bottom line.

Let's Think about Your Bottom Line

I'm not talking about how you look in jeans; I'm talking about how many pairs of jeans you can afford. Unless you've got a trust fund or have won the lottery, your salary is going to determine your buying power.

Obviously, your Inner Bitch wants you to give your salary some careful consideration. If you've chosen a particular career path (or even if you haven't), you know what kind of job you want to get, and you prepare yourself to get that job. You study the right things; you create a resume designed to show that you've got the right skills, yadda yadda yadda. In other words, you do the footwork before you get the job so that you *can* get the job.

This same concept applies to your salary. Your Inner Bitch knows that the best time to think about your bottom line is before you get a job.

Information is power, so do your research. What's the salary range for a position like this? What's a standard benefits package for the industry, and do most companies in the industry give common additional compensation such as stock options and bonuses (believe me, this matters). Do an online search on one of the websites that provides this kind of information. You may even want to invest in a personalized report that will take into consideration your geographic location, level of education, experience, and so forth. Talk to recruiters and people at industry organizations in your field. You might even want to call some people who have jobs like the one you want and ask them if they'd be willing to give you a ballpark estimate of their salaries.

Know when to talk about the M-word. Never be the first to bring up salary in an interview. Your job during the interview is to make yourself irresistible. That way your potential employer will want to do what it takes to make you want to join their team. Of course, they'll ask (they always do), so be ready to spin the conversation in your favor. Let the interviewer know that salary is important and that you want to lay the groundwork for determining what would be appropriate by learning everything you can about their expectations for the person who ends up in the job. If they push for an answer, talk standard industry ranges, not specific numbers.

When they offer you the job, they'll probably mention a salary. Never say yes to either right away (even if the money is really good). This is your opportunity to negotiate the deal you actually want, so now is the time to ask for either more money or some little extras, such as being able to work from home one day a week, more vacation time, a better title, tuition reimbursement (if that's not a standard benefit they offer), or a shorter waiting period before you're eligible to enroll in the company's 401(k) plan.

Your Inner Bitch wants you to remember that the worse they can say is no, and if what you're asking for is reasonable, the chances are that they'll say yes. If they don't say yes, and they rescind your offer, then remember that if they didn't think you were worth every penny during the courtship, they probably wouldn't change their minds over the long haul.

Raise the Ante

What if you're already in a job and you know you deserve a salary increase? Well, your Inner Bitch knows that the best time to ask for a raise is right after you've had a big success at work.

"Oh, no need for that! I'm sure my boss will remember this when it's time for my performance review," you say.

Well, who wrote that rule? And think about this—by performance review time, there's usually a budget in place; a budget that includes things like salaries and raises and things of that ilk. In other words, at that point it's too late to negotiate a salary bump on your terms. Wouldn't you rather have your boss have to build her budget using your new, improved salary? I think you would.

So, how do you get that bigger and better-than-ever salary? Your Inner Bitch wants you to apply the same careful consideration to getting the right raise as you would to negotiating the right salary and follow the same steps.

When you apply for a job, you and your prospective employer know that you're going to be talking money. Nobody likes to be ambushed (it makes them defensive and inclined to saying things like "no, no, no"), so it's a good idea to give your boss a heads-up that you want to discuss a raise. "But you just said the best time to ask for a raise is when I've had big success!" Yes, I did. These things aren't mutually exclusive. Your boss knows you've done well, and you know you've done well, so while the blush is still on the rose, say something like, "I'm really pleased that I landed that huge account. Since I just brought in X amount of money for the company, I think now is a good time to discuss my compensation. When can we sit down?"

Arm yourself with the facts, and be ready with documentation. Keep a record of your accomplishments, and don't be afraid to pull it out during your negotiation session. By the way, showing up on time every day is not an accomplishment, it's a given. And nobody deserves a raise because their rent went up or they just bought a new car; if your reasons for asking for a bump aren't related to business, you've got no business asking.

Practice makes perfect, so it's a good idea to call on one of your outside team members for a little "show me the money" role-playing. This is especially important for those of us who have even a remnant of Toxic Niceness floating around our psyches (that is, every one of us). Make sure that whoever is playing your boss throws you a couple of curve balls so you're ready for anything.

Remember that *no* is probably not the final answer. Even if your boss doesn't pony up the cash, ask for something else. What else is there? Let's think about that.

Hidden Assets

Money, of course, is not the only reward available to us. Whether you're negotiating your compensation package for a new job or for a raise, consider some of the other components that add value to your bottom line. For example:

❋ Time is a valuable commodity. Consider asking for more vacation time or flextime.

❋ If they're available, ask for stock options.

❋ Quid pro quo. If you travel for work, who gets the frequent flyer miles? How about getting the company to pay for some training, or membership in an industry organization?

No matter what you're negotiating, remember that your Inner Bitch knows you're worth it.

Taking Care of Business, Inner Bitch Style:

Remember that there's a lot of truth to the saying, "It's just business, it ain't personal." So the next time someone calls you "bitch" for insisting on excellence from yourself, your coworkers, and your direct reports, give yourself a pat on the back. A man would.

Chapter Ten
If You're the Boss, You're the Bitch

This Is Not a Popularity Contest

One of the concepts introduced in *Getting in Touch with Your Inner Bitch* was this:

"If we ask those who report to us to do their job well, and that means they have to work harder than they did before, they will probably call us 'bitch.'

"If those people who report to us do not do their job and we take them to task for that, they will call us 'bitch.'

"If we have taken those people to task and they still do not do their job, we will undoubtedly be more firm with them the second time we talk to them. They will definitely call us 'bitch.'

"Here's the simple truth: No matter how nicely we ask, if we are the boss, we are the bitch.

"What's the important part of that homily? We are the boss."

Being the boss isn't always easy. Being the boss isn't always fun. But most of the time being the boss beats the heck out *not* being the boss. For instance, here's a dirty little secret that most bosses will deny with all their might: when you're the boss, you do less actual work than when you're in the trenches. This isn't to say bosses don't work hard; lots of them do work hard. It's just that the work of the boss is less about producing such things as widgets, copy blocks, pots and pans—whatever a particular enterprise is involved in producing—and more about *managing* the production of whatever it is being produced. In other words, the boss has to lead everyone else toward a specific destination.

Let's think about that for a moment, shall we?

At its most basic, being the boss is sort of like being the cat wrangler: it requires big picture thinking, making sure everyone involved is heading in the right direction (and once that destination is reached, they have to decide where to go next).

Would you want to try to get your coworkers to do anything? Considering how hard it is to get most groups to agree on where to eat lunch, which they *want* to do. On second thought, being the boss might not sound like all that much fun after all. And given that most of the boss's day is spent bossing people around, it's a pretty sure bet that if you're the boss, people are going to resent you—even if you're just doing your job. In other words, if you are the boss, you are the bitch.

If you are the boss (or just want to be), your Inner Bitch wants you to embrace this fact. And she wants to remind you that being the boss is not the same thing as campaigning for Most Popular, although I've had plenty of bosses I liked quite a bit, and you probably have, too.

Your Inner Bitch knows that there are bad bosses, good bosses, really good bosses, and great bosses. If you are the boss, your Inner Bitch wants you to be the best boss you can be. So let's think about what that means.

The Boss
No One Wants to Be

It's easy to spot a bad boss, right? Bad bosses are unapproachable or unavailable. They're not supportive or even actively denigrate their teams. They're clueless; they play favorites; they make truly unreasonable demands (as opposed to demands that are reasonable, but because the boss is asking the demand seems unreasonable); and the list goes on and on. Your Inner Bitch knows that none of this is very useful, and it inevitably creates a losing cycle of poor morale, low levels of motivation, lack of productivity (no one wants to go the extra mile for a boss who only finds fault, after all), and threats being made about hammers and hatchets being dropped.

The tricky thing about bad bosses, however, is this: the worst boss might be one of the most like-able people around. You know the type. She's so adept at bending to please that she makes master yogis look inflexible, but in the process someone else (usually her staff) pays the price. I once had a boss, Lisa, whose immersion in Toxic Niceness was so complete that she couldn't say no to any request, no matter how ridiculous the request might be. Now I have to admit that I took advantage of this myself, for example, the time that I decided to take advantage of a special offer on a weekend getaway to the Bahamas—leave Thursday, come back Monday, airfare and hotel included for a really reasonable price. The fact that I made the decision to go on Wednesday was an inconvenient detail, but knowing that she was a pushover, I went into Lisa's office and asked if she'd mind if I took the next few days off. "Not a problem," she replied, even though company policy required that you give at least a little notice. "You've been working really hard, so a little break will probably do you a world of good!"

At that moment I thought Lisa might just be the best boss I'd ever had. But was she? Let's think about that. Did she ask if I'd made plans for how my work would be getting done while I was gone? Nope. Did she take into consideration whether or not my absence would affect any of my coworkers? I don't think so. Was I the only person in the department who got away with this kind of (admittedly) unprofessional behavior? Not by a long shot. And since Lisa also couldn't say "no" to anyone further up the chain of command, we were constantly being given last-minute projects with insanely tight deadlines. All of which created problems. Our department was constantly having to play catch up with ongoing projects because even when we had one of those "special projects," Lisa would give one of us a little time off or permission to leave early every day or . . . well, let's just say we functioned in a constant state of anarchy and disorganization. The rate of attrition was outrageous—people would leave after just a few months—and the worst part was that Lisa couldn't figure out why.

"I don't understand why we can't keep a team together. I work really hard to try to make everyone happy," she said to me one day.

"Maybe that's the problem," I suggested. But

Lisa waved that idea away like it was a bug.

The situation came to a head when the new EVP of marketing decided that the company needed a new look. He called a meeting of the creative department managers to discuss whether it was possible to develop a new branding initiative—a new logo, new images, the whole nine yards—in three months. Most of us shook our heads, but before we could speak Lisa blurted out, "Not a problem! We can do that!"

"Great!" said the EVP. "I want to see some proposed designs next week!"

"Are you kidding?" one of us asked Lisa as we filed out of the conference room. "How are we supposed to do that and get our usual work done?"

"I'll just have to figure out how to make it work," she said, going into her office and closing the door. She emerged a few hours later with a plan that involved everyone working weekends and four extra hours every day for the duration.

"I got management to agree to let us order lunch and dinner every day," she announced proudly. Eyes were rolled.

The project got done, but four members of our department quit. "I just can't keep working like this," one of them said when she announced her resignation. "I mean, it's great that she's so nice, but her lack of backbone is grinding me to a pulp."

Fortunately, at this point Lisa admitted that Toxic Niceness was making her a bad boss, and she decided to dedicate herself to becoming a good boss (or at least a better boss).

Better Bossing through Thinking

Lisa's first step on the pathway to better bossing was to get herself a bossing mentor. Everyone was a little surprised when she picked a man at her own level on the management scale, a guy

(Jim) known for being something of a hard-ass. Jim also had a reputation for being very fair and for getting great results from his department. Hardly anyone ever quit, and if they did, it was always because the opportunity was irresistible. "I figure I need to learn from a master," Lisa explained to him. "So, will you help me?"

"Why?" This was Jim's usual response to a request. Fortunately, Lisa was ready with an answer.

"Because people in my department clearly aren't happy, and I've got to turn things around or I might lose my job," she said.

"Okay. Start by exchanging that word 'happy' for one that actually pertains to business," he said. "Your focus shouldn't be on making your staff happy, because being the boss isn't a popularity contest. Your focus should be on figuring out what they need to be effective. And you clearly aren't doing that."

Ouch.

Fortunately, Lisa knew Jim was right. So, once a week they would go out to lunch to discuss what was going on in the company and how that might affect their departments. As Jim explained, thinking about the big picture was the first step in good management. Then he suggested that Lisa needed to figure out some way to circumvent what he called her "knee-jerk yes." He told her, "You have to think about how whatever someone is asking you for is going to affect everything else. Someone wants time off, which means either someone else has to do his or her work, or the work just doesn't get done. The folks upstairs want you to execute on their latest big idea, you have to think about if you have everything you need to make it happen."

"So, I should just say no to everyone?" Lisa asked.

"No. You just have to think before you say yes.

You're a manager, so you are the intersection where your staff and upper-management meet. So you have to handle the traffic coming from both sides. Your goal should be to make sure the traffic flows smoothly. Thinking about something is just like the yellow light on a traffic signal."

That afternoon I walked into Lisa's office to ask if I could hire four freelancers to deal with the fact that our department was down four people. Expecting the usual, "sure, go ahead," I was shocked when Lisa put a hand over her mouth before saying, "Let's think about the best way to handle the workload first. Figure out how many freelancers you need and for how long, then we'll discuss it, okay?"

See what happened there? Lisa didn't say no, but she also didn't say yes. I got my freelancers, but only two because, after we analyzed what our real needs were, we realized that some of the work could be shifted onto other people in the department. "But if we get any more projects, we'll readdress the situation," Lisa concluded.

Lisa's next step was to hang a calendar in our conference area to chart our projects and who had scheduled time off. Whenever someone asked for a day off, she consulted the calendar before giving the green light. But she used it to manage her boss, too. When he came up with yet another big idea, Lisa asked him to join her in the conference room, pointed to the calendar, and said, "We can do it, but as you see we're operating at our maximum capacity right now, so you're going to have to either help me move something onto a back burner or sign off on bringing in freelancers."

We didn't cheer, because that wouldn't have been professional.

Aiming for Greatness

Great bosses inspire. They may be demanding, and they certainly can be challenging. They may even be unreasonable at times (or seem to be), but they also drive us to do our best, come up with creative solutions to the issues we're facing, and provide the kind of support we need to develop those solutions. And they acknowledge our hard work.

It almost goes without saying that great bosses—both male and female—are in touch with their Inner Bitch.

According to the Center for Women's Business Research website, women owners of $1-million-plus businesses were more likely to have started their companies rather than have purchased, inherited, or acquired in some other way. Now that's what your Inner Bitch calls women doing it for themselves!

Chapter Eleven
Solo Flights

Your Inner Bitch knows that, for some of us, the true definition of success is owning our own business. One has to admire the Entrepreneurial Bitch—she has a vision; she has the courage to take on the challenge of building something from nothing (or very little); and she has the freedom to finally do things her own way. She's probably also exhausted.

But if being the boss is really your goal, Your Inner Bitch wonders what's stopping you?

"Well, isn't owning your own business a little, um, *risky?*"

Sure, but in the immortal words of Ronny Cammerari, "Why you wanna sell your life short?

Playing it safe is just about the most dangerous thing a woman like you could do."

Your Inner Bitch wants you to grab all that life has to offer with both hands—and that includes risks. So let's look at how some Entrepreneurial Bitches have taken charge of their professional lives.

Accidental Take-Offs

Sometimes going solo happens almost by mistake. You'll be plodding along in a job you don't hate when all of a sudden opportunity drops in your lap. The choice to grab hold and take the ride is yours, as is the responsibility for recognizing that it is, indeed, opportunity and not just a crazy idea.

For example, my friends Tina and Louise spent years working at a well-known home accessories store. There were things they loved about their jobs: being surrounded by tasteful design, setting up displays, getting to know the customers, the employee discount. But working in retail has its downside: the hours can be long; the pay is, well, let's just say that the employee discount only goes so far; and when there aren't a lot of customers it can get pretty boring. During one of those little dry spells, Tina showed Louise some placemats she'd bought when she was visiting her best friend in the country. "Aren't these great? I found them at a village fair; they were made by some women who are trying to raise money to help send a girl to college."

"Oh, they'd be perfect with those plates you've been thinking about! Let's see," Louise grabbed two of the placemats and made up a little display with plates Tina was considering buying. While they were fiddling around with the table settings, a customer came in, took one look at the display and asked if the placemats were in stock. When she found out they belonged to Tina, the customer offered to buy them from her for three times what Tina had paid. Tina didn't want to part with them, but she did offer to find out if there were any more available. After making a couple of calls, she tracked down one of the women who had made the placemats and asked if she could get six more.

Louise, who was standing close by, said, "Ask her if you can get twenty-four."

"Why?" Tina asked, covering the mouthpiece.

"Because if that woman wants them, other people will, too," Louise said. "And we can sell them for a lot more here than she'd get selling them in a booth at some fair. Offer her more if we can get twenty-four."

To make a long story short, Tina and Louise ended up not only selling all twenty-four of the placemats; they also got orders for more—and requests for more table setting options, like runners and whole tablecloths. Then Tina had the idea of offering all this stuff in custom colors and fabrics, and she and Louise researched how to get funding through state-sponsored grants to supplement their initial investment (which was something like $500). Within a year, she and Louise had opened their own shop and had a thriving website where they sold the items handmade by the original crafters, and they expanded their suppliers by starting a company that employs women who were rebuilding their lives after being homeless. "All of a sudden we're entrepreneurs who are able to provide opportunity to other women," Louise told me, still amazed at the changes that have taken place in her life and in Tina's. Of course, they had to give up some things, such as steady paychecks, company-sponsored health insurance, and the degree of security that comes from being employed by an established organization. But both of them wake up every day excited to go to work.

"And it's all because I took a weekend off and

found some cool placemats," Tina said.

The truth is, it's all because Louise and Tina recognized opportunity and went with it, responding to each challenge as it came up and just making their business happen.

Of course, your Inner Bitch knows that there's also something to be said for approaching going solo with a little more planning.

"It's a Business—Plan"

One woman I know—I'll call her Jean—always knew that she wanted to have her own business, she just didn't know what that business would be. Even in college, the idea of being an entrepreneur lurked just under the surface. So she decided to get an MBA and see where that got her, and after graduation she got a job working in marketing. Being really smart and a true workhorse, she quickly rose through the ranks to become a director, but she wasn't really happy with her situation.

"The secret of success in life is...
to be ready for...
opportunity when it comes."

—Benjamin Disraeli

"I just couldn't see the point in someone else profiting from my hard work," she explained. So she started planning.

The first step was establishing a budget so she could build a nest egg. The second was to make a list of businesses she might want to own, including such obvious ideas as a marketing agency and some really wacky ones (like a cotton candy concession at an amusement park). Then one day she was sitting in a coffee bar enjoying a latte and a little people-watching when it hit her: she wanted to own a coffee bar. In fact, she wanted to own *this* coffee bar, which was right down the street from her house. There were a couple of problems with this idea: the first being that someone else already owned it; the second being that she didn't know anything about the coffee business. So Jean asked the owner for a job working on the weekends and learned the basic stuff—for example, how to make espresso drinks and other little details.

At the end of a year, she had gained some basic knowledge, and all the money she made in tips and wages went into the nest egg. That's when she made her move, quit her job, and started managing the coffee shop, which helped fill in the gaps in her knowledge, because she was in charge of things such as ordering, scheduling, and more. All the while, Jean kept an eye out for an opportunity to make her move into owning the coffee bar, which arose when the landlord decided to raise the rent on the space.

"I can't afford that," the coffee bar owner said. "I'll have to shut down." But Jean had been paying attention to the fact that rents were rising for commercial space in the area, and because she knew that the location was ideal, she had developed a business model that made allowances for the higher rent. So, after her boss shut down, she rented the space herself, did some remodeling and opened for business.

Now this is where Jean's ambition to open her own coffee bar put her in an awkward position. To some minds she'd taken advantage of her boss to learn about the business, and since the customers loved that coffee bar and loved the original owner, they decided to boycott the new business. But Jean was in touch with her Inner Bitch, and she knew the truth to that old saying, "It ain't personal, it's business." And she knew that there were enough people who needed a caffeine fix (and didn't care who provided it) to keep her in business. Now, years later, she's moved to a new location right down the street with more parking and space to expand the business so she can offer more than just coffee. There are still some people who boycott the place, but there are plenty of others who come in every day. And Jean has what she always wanted—her own business.

From Humble Beginnings...

One notable woman who took a risk was Miss Lillian Vernon, who had the innovative idea of turning some of the money people gave as wedding presents into a business—you know, just a little something to keep her occupied and bring in some cash while she stayed home with the kids.

This is a fairly famous story, actually, but there are still plenty of lessons to be learned from it—some of which I had an opportunity to hear from the source when I worked at Miss Vernon's eponymous company. The basics are:

❖ Miss Vernon (and it's always Miss Vernon, even though her last name wasn't Vernon at all) decided that people might want some snazzy personalized belt buckles and handbags, so she took out a little ad in the back of *Seventeen* magazine offering those items at a very reasonable price.

✽ Miss Vernon was right. She got orders for $32,000 worth of merchandise.

✽ Miss Vernon parlayed those belt buckles and wallets into a multimillion-dollar company. And she became a major player—for instance, in recognition of her support for New York University (which she attended for two years before leaving to get married), the University established the Lillian Vernon Center for International Affairs in her honor. And she served on the boards of such august organizations as the Kennedy Center and Lincoln Center. In addition, she received awards such as the Ellis Island Medal of Honor, the Big Brothers Big Sisters National Hero Award, and the Direct Marketing Hall of Fame Award.

According to the Women's Business Research website,

"Women business owners have three top goals: to enjoy their daily work, increase profitability, and have the freedom to put into practice their own approach to work."

In other words, the lady took some risks (like being among the first American business owners to go to Asia for her products), she played by her own rules (how many other women started businesses at their kitchen tables in the 1950s?), and it paid off. One thing about Miss Vernon (and I say this with all due respect): that woman was in touch with her Inner Bitch. She understood that she was the boss; she was justifiably proud of what she accomplished; and she used her position as a business leader to help other women build successful careers. Of course, she was also a force to be reckoned with, holding herself and her employees to very high standards—no apologies, no excuses.

In other words, she was a success.

Appendix A

10 Tips for Getting the Career You Want

1. Make sure that your career ladder is leaning against "the right wall." What does this mean, exactly? It means that your Inner Bitch knows you need to pick the right career, at the right time. Whether you're just starting out or you've put in some time already, building the career you want requires that you spend your work days doing something that you enjoy.

Ideally, that means that at least some of the time *work* will feel like *play*.

❄ ❄ ❄

2. Know what you want, and be willing to do what it takes to get it. This doesn't mean ruthlessly going after your career goals. It just means that you accept that . . .

❄ ❄ ❄

3. There's nothing wrong with ambition.

❄ ❄ ❄

4. Plan your work, and work your plan. As Mary Kay Ash once said, "Those who are blessed with the most talent don't necessarily outperform everyone else. It's the people with follow-through who excel." Your Inner Bitch knows that having a road map is the surest way to reach the destination called *success*.

�֍ �֍ ✖

5. Practice mental yoga—be flexible. Sure, you may start out in marketing, but that doesn't mean you won't decide to shift gears at some point and decide that being a midwife is your true calling.

✖ ✖ ✖

6. Build your team, then use them.

✖ ✖ ✖

7. Take your vacation days.

✖ ✖ ✖

8. Act as if you were already there. Your Inner Bitch wants you to.

✖ ✖ ✖

9. Mistakes will happen—deal with them head-on.

❅ ❅ ❅

10. "Don't live down to expectations. Go out there and do something remarkable."
—Wendy Wasserstein

❅ ❅ ❅

BONUS TIP: Know the difference between you and your career.

Appendix B
The Writing on the Wall

No, this isn't a warning of dire conse-
quences. This appendix refers, of course,
to inspirational little sayings your Inner Bitch
thinks would be helpful to post somewhere
you'll see them throughout the day. Photocopy
any of these that work for you—or go wild and
create your own!

*It's easier to apologize than to ask for permission.
Think about this the next time you're considering
a bold maneuver.*

"If at first you don't succeed,
destroy all evidence that you tried."
—Susan Ohanian

Screw 'em if they can't take a joke.

If it's so lonely at the top, why aren't the boys
up there asking us to join them?

"Act as if it were impossible to fail."
—Dorothea Brand

"One-size-fits-all" doesn't work with success any more than it does with clothes.

Anyone who will not help you get to the top certainly isn't going to help keep you there.

You say I'm a bitch like that's a bad thing. . . .

I don't need to know everything.
I have people for that.

Elizabeth Hilts has had some jobs she'd like to forget, some jobs she's loved, and some jobs that were simply a means to an end (like, oh, survival). She currently works and lives in Connecticut, remaining open and ready for the next opportunity.